A Glimpse of
OLD HAM AND PETERSHAM

Written and compiled by

VANESSA FISON

FOREWORD BY SIR DAVID WILLIAMS

A century ago Ham and Petersham were sparsely populated Surrey villages, dominated by Ham House and Sudbrook Park. Even after all the building since then Ham and Petersham are more open, greener and more attractive than almost anywhere else in Greater London. We have Richmond Park on the east, the Thames and its riverside open space on the west, and Petersham Common woods and Petersham Meadows to the north. These green boundaries define our community very clearly.

Vanessa Fison's fascinating book shows what a rich legacy we have locally. Most of the historical photos show places that are still recognisable today. Her extensive research has produced a compact and very readable record of important aspects of the history of Ham and Petersham.

Vanessa is one of several researchers, historians and collectors who have been recording and publicising our local legacy. She also had a prominent role locally chairing the Ham and Petersham Association for several years. I won't forget her successful campaign to persuade Richmond Council to manage and improve the Ham House avenues, part of our 17th century legacy. As both a ward councillor and the Leader of the council at the time I was happy to persuade my colleagues that she was right.

There is more interest in the history of our attractive community than ever before, and the diligent work represented in this book adds to everyone's knowledge of Ham and Petersham.

Introduction and Acknowledgements

Much of the history of Ham and Petersham has already been told elsewhere and in my book *The Matchless Vale, The Story of Ham and Petersham and their People*. Indeed, some of the pictures in *A Glimpse of old Ham and Petersham* will have been seen before and may be familiar. There are however many new ones and some of them are remarkable in that they are over 100 years old. Reproducing them in a large format has made it possible to examine them more closely and to see some fascinating details.

Particular thanks are due to Keith Mulberry who is such an expert on local social history and has helped me out on a number of occasions; to David Foll who has edited the book with such a scholarly eye; to David Yates whose advice and recommendations are always so sound. I am grateful to the Local Studies Library at Richmond and to Sir David Williams for agreeing to allow me to reproduce some of the photos from their collections.

I should be pleased to hear from readers who have any evidence to add to the research I have done on the images and text in this book.

Vanessa Fison
2017

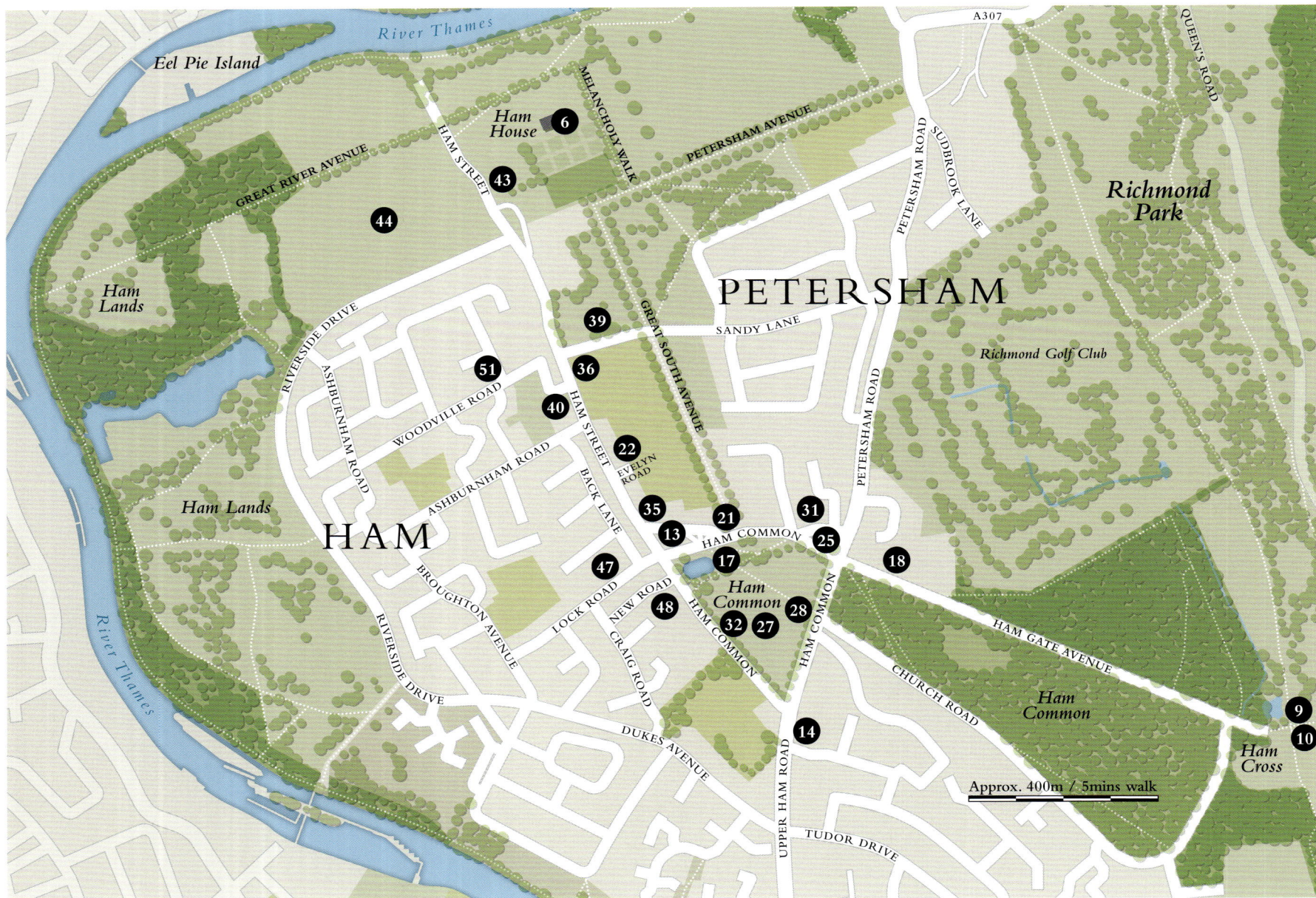

River Thames

Eel Pie Island

Ham House **6**

Melancholy Walk

Petersham Avenue

A307

Queen's Road

43

44

Great River Avenue

Ham Street

Ham Lands

Richmond Park

PETERSHAM

Richmond Golf Club

Petersham Road

Sudbrook Lane

Sandy Lane

39

Great South Avenue

Riverside Drive

Ashburnham Road

51

36

Woodville Road

40

Ham Street

22

Evelyn Road

Ashburnham Road

Back Lane

Ham Lands

HAM

35

13

21

Ham Common

31

25

18

Petersham Road

47

Broughton Avenue

Lock Road

New Road

17

Ham Common

48

Ham Common

28

32 **27**

Ham Common

9

10

Riverside Drive

Craig Road

Dukes Avenue

Ham Common

Church Road

Ham Gate Avenue

Ham Common

Ham Cross

River Thames

14

Upper Ham Road

Tudor Drive

Approx. 400m / 5mins walk

— 4 —

KEY TO MAP FOR HAM

The page numbers of each page given above are also shown on the map opposite

HAM HOUSE

The scene opposite was painted in watercolour by Thomas Rowlandson in the early 1800s. Rowlandson was a prolific artist and caricaturist, who was particularly known for his apt and comic images of life in Georgian England. It is thought that this painting, entitled *Lord Dysart treating his Tenantry*, depicts Sir Wilbraham Tollemache, the 6th Earl of Dysart, seen here toasting and entertaining his tenants in the meadow beyond the terrace and entrance gates at the north front of Ham House. A convivial personality, who served in the Navy and then the Army, the 6th Earl was much loved by the people of Ham and Petersham for his amiable and benevolent character. The gathering is jovial, the ale is being decanted from barrels into jugs by two hard-working individuals on the extreme right.

When Sir Wilbraham succeeded to the earldom in 1799, he opened up the house to the river. Previously, the forecourt was enclosed but he demolished the front wall and re-positioned some of the 'heads of lead', as they were known, in niches along the front façade of the house. The heads are a series of busts of Roman Emperors and Kings, cast in lead and painted to resemble stone. A ha-ha was dug on each side of the iron entrance gates with stone piers, and he built a new low wall with pineapple finials along its length. The railings along the balustrade that are there today did not come for about another 100 years, when they were erected by the 9th Earl.

Sir Wilbraham also commissioned the reclining statue of the River God in the centre of the forecourt, which was designed by John Bacon and moulded in Coade stone. The figure is almost 3 metres long and is cast in a single mould. The pineapples along the wall were also of Coade stone. Eleanor Coade, born in 1733, was the daughter of a wool merchant from Exeter; she invented the artificial stone that bears her name, which she produced from her factory in Lambeth. A mouldable artificial stoneware that stands the greatest tests of weathering and erosion, Coade stone was a highly popular medium for the creation of monuments of this type at the time.

THE DYSARTS

Sir William John Manners Tollemache, the 9th Earl of Dysart (1859-1935) resided at Ham House at the turn of the 20th century and he was the last Dysart and Lord of the Manor to live there. His father, Sir William Lionel Felix Tollemache, predeceased his grandfather the 8th Earl and so he inherited the Dysart estates, which included almost 500 acres in Ham in 1899.

The 9th Earl's marriage did not last long and there were no children. The Countess apparently found him difficult to live with and one day ordered a carriage that took her to Kensington in London and she never returned. He didn't seem to mind, only resenting her failure in not telling him! Partially blind and of a nervous temperament, towards the end of his life he became very deaf, but his afflictions did not prevent him from maximising his assets. He modernised Ham House and installed central heating and electricity. Apart from this, since the end of the 17th century when it was the home of the Earl's ancestor Elizabeth Murray, Countess of Dysart and Duchess of Lauderdale, little else has changed.

At his death, Dysart owned 70% of the houses in Ham and Petersham, but his heirs were unable to maintain the estate. Coupled with death duties and the onset of the Second World War, the family were forced eventually to donate Ham House to the National Trust in 1948. Most of the houses that were owned by the Dysarts were auctioned off in 1949.

This delightful oil painting opposite of the Earl of Dysart's family in Richmond Park by William Frederick Wither-ington (1785-1865) is one of many images of Richmond Park belonging to the Hearsum Collection at Pembroke Lodge. Unfortunately, the work is not dated, but from the dress and style of the figures it is thought that it may have been painted at the time of Lionel Tollemache, the 8th

Earl of Dysart. The young people depicted could well be the 8th Earl with two of his younger brothers, the Hon Frederick James Tollemache and the Hon Algernon Gray Tollemache. The young men were known to be handsome and, a typical Tollemache trait, were all over six feet tall. Frederick and Algernon became trustees for their brother managing Ham House and the estates for him. The 8th Earl was by all accounts an eccentric and peculiar character. He lived the life of a recluse and miser at 34 Norfolk Street in the Strand and never visited Ham House. He accumulated vast wealth, which in his will he left in trust for his grandson the 9th Earl. His brothers, Frederick and Algernon, along with Frederick's son-in-law, the Hon Charles Hanbury-Tracy, who became 4th Lord Sudeley in 1877, were trustees and it wasn't until the 9th Earl was 40 years old that he personally took control of the estates.

It is possible that the gathering may be seated somewhere close to Ham Cross (see page 11). At first glance one might think that the steeple depicted in the painting was that of St Matthias Church, situated on Richmond Hill. But it is an illusion. The church was not completed until 1857 when the artist was 72 and it is thought that he painted the work earlier in his life. The architect of this notable church built in the Victorian Gothic Style was Sir George Gilbert Scott, who spent the last years of his life at the Manor House on Ham Street.

RICHMOND PARK

In 1637, Charles I enclosed an area of 2,500 acres, now Richmond Park, which included land from Petersham and a considerable part of Ham. He then built a two-metre-high, 10-mile wall to surround it, for his hunting pleasure. In 1751 George II's daughter, Princess Amelia, who was Park Ranger at the time, removed the ladder-stiles which provided public access to prevent the crowds that generally turned up on hunting days. She allowed entry by ticket only, to personally selected guests.

Despite a spirited defence of public access in the mid-1750s by the local Richmond hero, the brewer John Lewis, a degree of restricted access to the Park continued until well into the middle of the 19th century, and carriages and horseback riders were only admitted with a signed card of admission.

There was a ladder-stile next to Ham Gate, which was erected in 1758 and was still in existence in 1850.

This admittance card, dated 1841, has been signed by the 1st Viscount Sidmouth, Henry Addington, the former Prime Minister, who lived at White Lodge and was Deputy Park Ranger at the time. In this photo, c.1900, a 'fly' or carriage approaches the hill towards Ham Cross from Ham Gate. At the time the photo was taken all restrictions to the Park had been lifted.

The Ham Gate to the Park at the end of Ham Gate Avenue is one of the original six entrances to the Park and dates back to the time of Charles I's enclosure.

In 1921 Ham Gate was widened somewhat, but it is still the narrowest entrance to the Park, with only a single

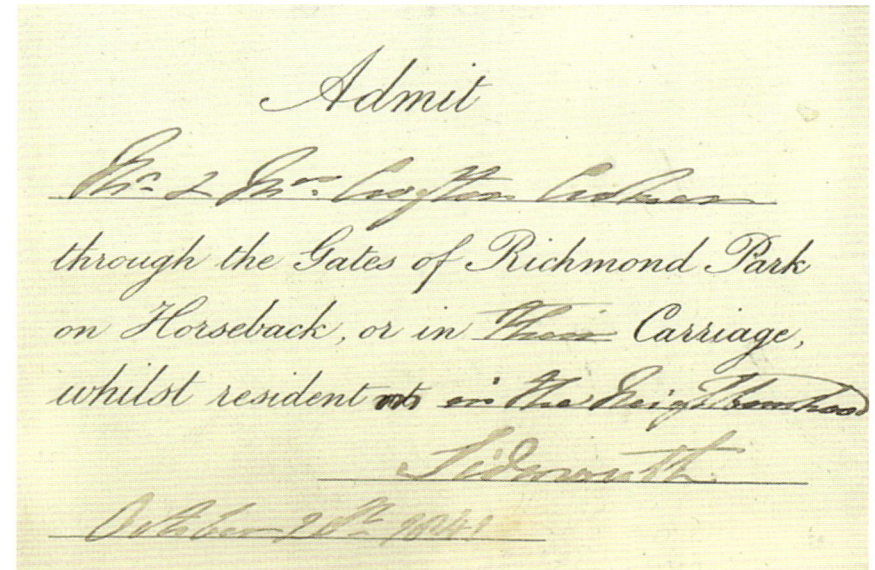

carriageway and one pedestrian entrance. At this time, the carriage gates were constructed in timber and had brick piers that were surmounted by gas lanterns. They were replaced by the existing wrought-iron gates but the piers and lanterns were retained. These are notable in that they are the only gates in the Park which are still to this day lit by gas. They glow gently with a soft parchment coloured light.

CORONATION CELEBRATIONS, 1911

When King Edward VII died, the coronation of his son, the new King George V and Queen Mary took place at Westminster Abbey on 22 June 1911. This is an extract taken from the diary of George V on the day of his Coronation:

'The Service in the Abbey was most beautiful and impressive, but it was a terrible ordeal. It was grand, yet simple & most dignified & went without a hitch. I nearly broke down when dear David (later Edward VIII) came to do homage to me, as it reminded me so much when I did the same thing to beloved Papa, he did it so well. Darling May looked lovely & it was indeed a comfort to have her by my side as she has been ever to me during these last 18 years'.

The village of Ham celebrated the event with a Coronation Procession, which was recorded by the Surrey Comet on 1 July 1911. Girls from the National Orphan Home (see page 30) dressed in white joined the National School, now (the Catholic) St Thomas Aquinas Church, on Ham Street, the building on the right of this photo, opposite. In brilliant sunshine, the 150 children carried large banners and flags, and were garlanded with flowers and wreaths. Most of them wear stout black lace-up boots with dark woollen stockings, typical Edwardian attire, which must have been very uncomfortable in the heat!

The headmaster of the National School, Mr Barnes, in his smart boater hat is on the right of the photo. They all marched across the Common, led by a massed fife and drum band, to an open-air service at St Andrew's Church, where they were joined by 80 school children from the Russell School in Petersham (see page 62). Hymns and the national anthem were sung, led by the Bishop of Kingston, Dr Cecil Hook (in his top hat in the photo on this page), and the vicar of St Andrew's, the Revd. James Pridie.

After the service at St Andrew's, the nine-year-old Joyce Anstruther, the granddaughter of Lord and Lady Sudeley of Ormeley Lodge, planted a Cedar tree on the Common, by Church Road at the corner of the Upper Ham Road. Twenty-eight years later, Joyce was to write the bestselling book *Mrs Miniver* under the pen name of Jan Struther, which was also made into the Academy award winning film. The ceremony was followed by patriotic speeches, and the 400 children from the two parishes were entertained to tea on the Common, where two large marquees had been erected. There was a Punch and Judy show and various sports, as well as a tug-of-war over Ham Pond. In the evening, there was dancing, and Chinese lanterns were hung on the trees. The day ended with a large firework display.

UPPER HAM ROAD

This photo, c.1920-30, is taken from near the Hand and Flower public house on the south side of Ham Common, and it shows the road to Kingston. On the left-hand side of the road to the east stood a large house known as the Elms, later Cairn House. The house was demolished to make way for the Parkleys housing development, which was completed in 1955-56.

The row of terraced cottages on the right are still familiar today although the large door has been changed to a shop window. On the wall above (where the two men are standing) is a sign for 'Warner', the decorators supply store. In the mid-1890s, William Warner was a local builder and wheelwright. It is thought that the narrow lane beyond these houses was named after him.

The building on the extreme left of the row is the Gate House, so called because there used to be a gate across this road which stopped animals, particularly cattle, straying off the Common. Other similar gates existed near the New Inn public house on Ham Common (erected in 1771 but removed 1892) and another close to the Ham Tap public house on Ham Street. The gate houses were Almshouses and the tenancy agreement was that the occupants operated the gates. The Gate House bears the inscription, 'Erected by the inhabitants of Ham and Hatch in 1771'.

Mrs Sarah 'Grannie' Morffew lived here for 40 years. She was the daughter of a charcoal burner. She died in 1892 at the age of 105 and was buried in the churchyard of St Andrew's. One of the old traditions at the Gate House which existed until the Second World War was known as 'Bringing in the Yule Log'. Traditionally a large log was dragged back home on Christmas Eve and brought to the fireplace to be lit with the remains of the previous year's log which had been carefully stored away. It was kept burning during the twelve days of Christmas. It was believed that this brought good luck to everyone in the house for the coming year.

Just out of view between the row of terraced houses and the Gate House and set back from the road, there used to be a beer house in the latter half of the 19th century, known as the Crown. There was also a skittle alley. A group of buildings next door were occupied by the Greenwood family for many years until well into the 20th century, and there was a dairy where Walter Greenwood, and then his son Earnest, produced bottled milk and had sheds for their cows. There are still descendants of the Greenwood family who live in Ham today. Beyond the Gate House in the photo, where the scene is still rural, the road narrows and curves around to the left. Now the Ham Parade of shops occupies both sides of the road.

HAM POND

Cattle grazed freely on Ham Common until the 1930s and drank from the Pond, which has always been a focal point of the village. It was a chief attraction for young children, and on Bank Holidays, tug-of-war competitions took place over the Pond with teams assembled from the neighbouring public houses. For many years, a firework display and bonfire were held on the Common on Guy Fawkes Day. Bull-frogs used to breed in the Pond and geese were plentiful.

This old coloured postcard of Ham Pond, dating from the late 19th century, shows the north-west side of the Common. From the left, partially obscured, is the Little House on the corner of New Road and Ham Common. It used to be called Laurel Cottage in the 1840s and then Ivycroft in the late 1890s and was the home of Sarah Smith, who wrote religious novels with a moral tone for children under the pen name of Hesba Stretton. She also contributed to *Household Words*, a weekly magazine that was edited by Charles Dickens in the 1850s.

Ensleigh Lodge, with its curious façade, was built in the early 1800s. Next to it, the oak-framed Malthouse was part of a large complex of buildings, which included the Malthouse Cottage as well as a farm called Home Farm behind the buildings. The Malthouse with its louvred and ventilated roof was worked by Joseph and Daniel Light, and the family supplied local brewers from as far afield as Guildford. In its heyday in the 19th century, a delicious smell filled the air as the cereal grains were converted into malt. It was pulled down in 1906 to make way for the straightening of Lock Road (see page 46). All that now remains is the white house with its mansard roof situated on the north side of Lock Road and the Malthouse Cottage on the south side of the road (obscured by Ensleigh Lodge in this postcard).

The Ham National School, now St Thomas Aquinas Church, with the two pitched roofs and steeple, is next; the high brick wall has now gone. On the right, to the left of the tree, the 3-storey Selby House, with its Queen Anne façade, can just be seen.

HAM GATE AVENUE

This is Ham Gate Avenue c.1900. It shows a very rural scene with chickens roaming freely as well as the old road or track to Ham Gate, the entrance to Richmond Park. Maybe the people in the photo are residents of Ormeley Lodge whose entrance gates can be seen on the left, or the nearby Sudbrook Lodge. Young sycamore trees line the road and they have now become a feature of the Avenue with their beautiful overhanging branches. However, they are in decline, many suffering from sooty bark disease and recently many have had to be felled. The area on each side of the Avenue, now known as Ham Common Woods, was less covered in undergrowth and trees one hundred years ago, and cattle grazed there up to the mid–1900s.

John Roque's map of the area (c.1746) shows a curved route from Ham to the Park, which may have been no more than a track. In 1817, a banker, Benjamin Barnard, at one time High Sheriff of the County of Surrey, who lived at Park Gate House adjacent to Ham Gate, employed local labourers to make a straight carriage way for easier vehicle access to the Park and his own house. The parish council minutes at that time show that the path was named 'Barnard's Footpath'. In 1861, it was named Park Road and in 1945 Richmond Borough Council changed the name again to Ham Gate Avenue at the time the road was first metalled or tarmacked.

THE GATEHOUSE, HAM COMMON

John Clifford says that this is a picture of his maternal grandfather, John Buckner, who died in 1963 and lived in Evelyn Road (see page 23). He was a father of seven children and was a gardener and horticulturist for most of his working life. In his retirement years, he worked in the garden of Mrs Barf's cottage on Ham Common, known as the Gatehouse, which can just be seen on the left. It is one of a pair of historic Gatehouse lodges on either side of the Great South Avenue leading to Ham House, built in the Jacobean style with Dutch gables in the late 17th century by the Dysarts. The two dwellings have a Grade II historic building listing and were probably built at the same time that the Avenues that surround Ham House were laid out.

On the right of the photo is Avenue Lodge which enclosed the eastern Gatehouse lodge within its boundary in 1892. Originally, the walks, as the Ham House Avenues were known, were ornamental and gravelled; the approach to Ham House was from the river to the north and to the west of the house via the stables on Ham Street. The three Avenues, the Great South Avenue, Petersham Avenue and Melancholy Walk were lined with Dutch Elm trees, which succumbed to disease in the late 1960s. They were subsequently replanted with the Lime trees that we see today. The John Roque map of c.1746 shows all the Avenues, including the Great River Avenue, which stretched from Ham House in a westerly direction, across Ham Lands to the river.

Evelyn Road

Built in about 1884, many of the tenants who came to live in the original eighteen houses on Evelyn Road had lived mostly on Ham Lane, now Ham Street, and worked as agricultural labourers on the farms in Ham or were in service. There were also gardeners, carpenters, dressmakers and laundresses, all finding work in the several larger houses in Ham. The houses on the north side of the street (to the left of the photo) were built first and all were fully occupied by 1891. They remain remarkably unchanged to the present day, retaining the original brickwork.

Notice the iron railings in this early 1900 photo: most of these were dismantled for the war effort (Second World War), although some of the railings at the end of the road still exist. Cows used to graze on the field beyond the houses, which was known as Brick Field, and is now the playing fields for Grey Court School. In the Second World War, an incendiary bomb was dropped in the field, perilously close to the houses, but caused no damage to them.

The parked cars we see today lining the street didn't come until the 1960s. Mr Buckle at no. 15 was the first on the road to own one. It would be fascinating to know how they managed in the 'two up, two down' houses with no inside lavatory and water having to be heated on the stove for baths in the kitchen. Bathrooms were added to the houses as late as the 1960s.

At the time of this photo, as many as seven people lived in one house including a lodger. John Robert Ridger, who lived at no. 10 (on the extreme right) and was the only owner occupier at this time, he was a carpenter. His wife Fanny opened a general shop and confectioner's on the street level in the early 1900s.

By 1891 a golf club had opened at Sudbrook Park and provided employment for several occupants of the road. Shadrack Hopkins, who lived at no. 18, was involved in the 1891 dispute with the Dysart trustees relating to the rights of the villagers of Ham to the Common (see William Harry Harland, page 46). He was one of those accused of the serious crime of felony, for cutting down notices that had been erected by the Dysart trustees forbidding the removal of gravel and of turf, and the killing of game without a licence, actions which the inhabitants of Ham claimed were their treasured and ancient rights. He was acquitted, along with his colleagues, much to the delight of his fellow villagers.

Members of the Whiting family lived in four separate houses on the road in 1891. The Whitings were agricultural labourers, brick layers and gardeners. Eileen Clifford (née Buckner), mother of John, (see page 20) has lived on the road all her life. The Buckners lived firstly at no. 4 and then at no. 9, where Eileen was born before moving across the road when she married Alfred Clifford, father of John, and moved in with his family at no. 10 where she still lives.

THE NEW INN, HAM COMMON

On 7th November 1886, a group of cyclists met at the New Inn public house after a weekend ride and over tea it was agreed that they would form themselves into a club. Members made a payment of 1s to join and the Bath Road Club was founded. In the late 19th century, the penny-farthing was also known as the 'high-wheeler', and was the first of its kind to be known as a 'bicycle'. The rider sat at the top of the front larger wheel axle and the cranks and pedals were fixed directly above this wheel. Mounting the penny-farthing required skill and practice. The name was taken from the penny and farthing coins – one much larger than the other, so that from the side it resembles a penny leading a farthing.

John Foley, the name on the front of inn on this early 1900's photo, right, is listed as being the landlord of the New Inn in the 1891 Kelly's Directory. There has been an inn on this site since the 17th century. The building that is still there today was built between 1756 and 1775. It was originally called the White Hart. In 1780 the name was changed to the Hobart Arms, most probably because George Hobart, 3rd Earl of Buckinghamshire, had a country 'villa' at the time across the other side of the Common in a house, long since demolished, situated between Langham House and Lawrence Hall, next to the Cassel Hospital. In 1822 the name reverted to its current name, the New Inn.

Far right, one of the first motor vehicles travelling down the Upper Ham Road towards the New Inn. This open-topped vehicle was fitted with a body style known as a 'tonneau', a fairly common body that was fitted to cars in

the early Edwardian period. There seems to be no registration number displayed on the rear of the vehicle, so this picture may have been taken before 1st January 1904 as this was the date the 1903 Motor Car Act came into force, requiring driver licensing and that all motor vehicles be registered at a cost of 5s and display number plates. The Act increased the speed limit for motorcars to 20 mph from the previous 14 mph.

It is interesting to note that when this photo was taken the Upper Ham Road ran up to the front door of the New Inn. The road was widened and straightened in 1957, the Upper Ham Road merging with the Petersham Road and passing the New Inn to the west.

The 'Age' Brighton Coach, Ham Common

The 'Age' crossing Ham Common from Brighton on its way to London. This coloured aquatint, dated 1852, was painted by William Joseph Shayer Jnr and engraved by Charles Hunt. Note St Andrew's Church, which was built in 1831 and can be seen in the distance on the far right of this print. In its heyday in the early 19th century, the four-horse coaches, conveying goods and passengers, proceeded at a gallop at eleven miles an hour. There was a regular service from Brighton to London and it was at that time the only means of long-distance transport. Stops were made at inns en route and sometimes passengers had to get out and walk up some of the steeper hills. Journey times were improved by the metallisation (tarmacking) of roads, but the increase of speed resulted in more accidents.

The golden age of the horse coach was eclipsed by the arrival of the 'Iron Horse' or steam railway. It never reached Ham and Petersham. The 'Age' was still in service until 1862. Charles G. Harper (see page 70), in his book *The Brighton Road, the Classic Highway to the South* first published in 1892, writes about the revived 'Age' in about 1852, then owned and driven by Henry Somerset, the 8th Duke of Beaufort and travelling on the road to London via Dorking and Kingston in the summer months.

THE TILLING OMNIBUS

This photo shows the Thomas Tilling 'Knifeboard' type horse bus or omnibus outside the Orange Tree public house, in Richmond on its way to Kingston, via Petersham and Ham in the early 1900s. Noticeable for the curving staircase at the rear and outside seating on the roof, the Knifeboard buses were designed to carry up to twenty-six passengers. Not particularly comfortable or cheap, the buses were convenient and very well used. One of London's oldest bus companies, Thomas Tilling was started in 1846. Tilling was born in 1825 in Hendon, Middlesex, and when he was 21 years old he set up as a 'jobmaster' with one horse and carriage which he drove himself. By 1849 he had progressed to the two-horse omnibus and by the end of the century there were more than a thousand buses on the streets in the Greater London area. It was Tilling's omnibuses that first stopped at prede-termined places and ran to a fixed timetable and he became very successful running the largest number of horse-powered vehicles, in the London area.

The ones that went along the Petersham Road every quarter of an hour started outside the Orange Tree public house on the Kew Road in Richmond and came via the Petersham Road and Ham Common (as the sign on the side of the bus shows). They ended at the Druid's Head in the Market Place, Kingston. As well as Tilling's own omnibuses, his horses ran hearses as well as fire engines. When he died in 1893, his two sons, Richard and Edward, took over the family business and the company was incorporated in 1897. By the early 1900s the company had 250 buses, which required 7,000 horses based at 500 different stables. In those days, route numbers were not used and the Tilling buses were painted predominantly green, using coloured boards and lettering to show passengers on which route a bus was running. Horse-led buses finally ceased to operate at the outbreak of the First World War, horses being in demand for war service in France. Open topped buses continued to operate along the Petersham Road until well after the Second World War. The seats inside faced each other down the length of the bus.

NATIONAL ORPHAN HOME, HAM COMMON

Right, five young girls from the National Orphan Home sitting on Ham Common in front of South Lodge, early 1900's. Opposite, an earlier coloured print of the building from the west, by Edward Collier. The National Orphan Home for girls was made possible by the purchase of the 3-acre site by John Minter Morgan, a philanthropist and author. He was the son and heir of a wealthy wholesale stationer, and in 1835 he bought the Morgan House Estate, on the west side of Ham Common, which now includes Cassel Hospital. He campaigned for universal free and progressive education and promoted the radical and unorthodox Alcott School and Concordium – a vegetarian and celibate commune of 'sacred socialists' with utopian ideals and religious principles. In 1849, as a result of the devastating national cholera epidemic he bought and converted this building on the north-east side of the Common into an orphanage for girls.

The orphanage gave a basic education as well as training to the girls to enable them to become domestic servants when they left at the age of 15. A leaflet describing the Home declared to 'receive them and provide for them, till of age to help themselves – to prepare them for usefulness in the world, and to train them in the path of Virtue and Religion'.

John Minter Morgan died and was buried at St Andrew's Church in January 1855. The orphanage was enlarged after his death and run by a management committee that was supported by voluntary contributions. It also took in many orphans from the Crimean War.

The building that is seen here provided accommodation for 120 girls and was completed in 1866. The orphanage continued in existence until 1922.

During the Second World War, South Lodge was a Community Centre, since then the building has been converted into residential flats.

Forbes House, Ham Common

One of the most historic houses in Ham, Forbes House on the west side of Ham Common, was once the home of the Gordon Forbes family and has seen many family tragedies in its long history. Gordon was the son of General Gordon Forbes of Gordon House, out of sight on this photo but further north on the same road. The General had lived on Ham Common for almost 50 years and died just short of his 90th birthday. His son Gordon also lived to a great age. He had a long career as a civil servant in India, retired at the age of 42 and returned home to live at Forbes House for the rest of his life. He died here in 1870 at the age of 87. He had two young children from his first marriage who died tragically on their return to England from India when the vessel they were sailing in was shipwrecked off the Cape of Good Hope. He then had a further twelve children with his second wife. Gordon was active in the local community and helped to establish St Andrew's Church in 1832 (up to this time there was no local parish church in Ham). He also was one of the founding members of the committee that was formed to manage the National Orphan Home (see page 30), and he helped to set up the first parochial schools in Ham. In a further tragedy, his three youngest children, Charles, Urquhart and Lushington, aged 4, 2 and 1 respectively, all died at Forbes House in November 1835, having contracted measles.

The ivy-clad extension on the right of the main building was a later addition to the house. At the time of this early 1900s photo, Forbes House was the home of Mrs Harry Warren Scott, whose eldest daughter by her first marriage, Cecilia Nina, married Claude George Bowes-Lyon, Lord Glamis (later Earl of Strathmore and Kinghorne) and became the grandmother of the late Queen Mother. Cecilia and Lord Glamis were married at St Peter's Church, Peter-sham in July 1881 and their wedding breakfast was held at Forbes House. Their eldest daughter, Violet Hyacinth Bowes-Lyon, was only 11 when she died here in October 1893. She had contracted diphtheria and was buried at St Andrew's Church. It is said that the late Queen Mother sometimes came to visit her grandmother at Ham Common when she was a child.

Mrs Scott lived at Forbes House until her death aged 86 in 1918. Her only unmarried daughter, Violet Cavendish-Bentinck, continued to live at Forbes House and carried out many charitable works in Ham. It was she who ran Gordon Hall in New Road (see page 49) and the Violet Home for Crippled Children in Lock Road (see page 46).

In 1935 the house as seen in this photo c.1900 was demolished and replaced with a rectangular-shaped building with two wings at each end. It became a welfare home to accommodate 44 elderly people and was finally demolished again in 1992 and rebuilt as the present neo-classical house by the architect Julian Bicknell.

Note the 'Victoria' tucked into the driveway on the left at what is now the garage of Langham Cottage, no, 12 Ham Common. These elegant, French horse-drawn carriages were popular amongst the more well-to-do families of the time. It had a raised driver's seat for the coachman, supported by an iron frame with a folding or 'calash' top.

On the right of the photo is Rose Cottage, the home, for many years, of the Lansdale family. It was demolished and replaced with a modern house in 2008 and is now called Rose House. On the far right is the Cottage which is attached to Flax Cottage. Originally called 'Noreena', the name was changed in the 1980s by the then occupant, Mrs Nobel, to Flax Cottage, as there were then acres of flax fields at the back of the house.

HAM STREET, SOUTHERN END

Right: a view of Ham Street facing north from a drawing by John Sanderson-Wells, c.1940, and far right, the same view in a photo taken about twelve years later in 1952.

This is the main street of the village which runs from Ham Common to the River Thames. It was known as Ham Lane until c.1860.

The Ham Brewery Tap is on the extreme right. It was built in 1934 and replaced an earlier building which was probably over four hundred years old. Beyond are the terraced houses nos. 12- 24 Ham Street, which are much the same today.

On the extreme left, barely visible, is a sign for the Crooked Billet. Originally this pub was situated at nos. 31 and 33 Ham Street, the tall, three-storey building on the west of the street now the Ham General Stores. It was rebuilt at nos. 13-23 Ham Street in 1935 and demolished in 1996, then replaced with a row of terraced houses.

After the Crooked Billet moved to its new location, the Ham General Stores building was converted into two shops, a butcher's and a general store that used to be known as Dunkley's after Dorothy and Harry Dunkley, who first had a shop on the other side of the road at no. 12 and moved here just after the Second World War. Now it is just one shop. Beyond in the distance can be seen Stokes Hall (now House). In 1972, this building was divided into two houses, Stokes House and the Bench.

Notice the lack of any parked cars in both images, compared to now! Also in the photo on the right, a familiar sight in those days, just a few years after the Second World War, was that of a man with just one leg walking along the pavement on crutches.

HAM STREET, NORTHERN END

Another view of Ham Street from a drawing by John-Sanderson Wells c.1940, further north towards the river at the corner of Sandy Lane, with the Royal Oak public house on the right. It is thought that the Royal Oak may originally have been an abattoir for Ham Manor Farm before it became an inn. Recent research by Keith Mulberry confirms that the inn has been a public house for some 200 years. The building lease was purchased by Thomas Yarrell in 1823 from the heirs of Thomas Paine, who was a prosperous tradesman from Richmond and descended from a long line of successful butchers. It appears that it became an inn sometime between 1823 and 1828 under Yarrell's ownership. It closed in 2011 and is now being converted into the new Ham Village Centre, the replacement for the Ham Working Men's Institute which used to be on New Road (see page 49). In the course of the renovations, the entrance to a bricked-up subterraneous passage was found in the cellar facing the Manor House.

Left, an assessed tax form, dated 1839 which was served on Mr Inskip, the tenant of the Royal Oak and signed by him and the collector of taxes. This form was amongst the papers for the inn that were passed on to the new owners of the Institute. It is interesting in that it shows the different types of tax that were payable to the government. The land tax was a tax on property, payable every quarter, by the tenant of a dwelling. The form shows that the land tax rate was 3s 7½p a quarter; 14s 6p a year.

Other assessed taxes were based on luxury items; the number of servants, carriages, horses and dogs etc. Although none of the other taxable charges listed on the form were applicable to the landlord of the inn, two of them are worthy of note, a tax on windows and a tax on hair powder.

The tax on windows in houses was first introduced in 1696 and replaced the hearth tax (introduced in 1662) which was charged on every inhabited dwelling. In order to assess the tax that was due, visits of the 'chimney men' – the assessors and collectors - used to take place. They had the right to enter a house to count the hearths. These visits had been unpopular as they were deemed to be an intrusion into the house of an Englishman. The tax was repealed in 1688 and shortly after replaced with the window tax. This tax was based on the number of windows in each house and was deemed to be less intrusive as it could be assessed from outside the house. It was still an unpopular tax and many householders bricked up some of their windows to reduce the amount they had to pay. The tax continued until it was repealed in 1851.

One of the more curious items on the list is the imposition of a tax on the wearing of hair powder. For some time, the French fashion of powdered hair had replaced fashionable wigs or *perruques*, though by the beginning of the 19th century this was largely confined to coachmen and footmen in service. The Royal family, their servants and clergymen with an income under £100 were exempt. The tax hastened the extinction of the fashion and the tax was repealed in 1869.

Sandy Lane

Sandy Lane, as its name suggests, used to be a narrow single track road without pavements. It runs from Ham Street to the Petersham Road. This view is taken from the west end, looking towards Petersham from the corner of Ham Street. Residents remember that early in the 1960s the road was still lined with mature trees with their canopies merging overhead to form a beautiful arch over the road from the Great South Avenue to Ham Street.

On the right of this photo, taken in 1952 is the exterior wall of one of the two small Royal Oak cottages that used to adjoin the public house to the north on Ham Street. Both the cottages were demolished in 1957. Beyond on the right were the grounds of Grey Court which were incorporated into the school, which opened in September 1956. The Royal Oak was threatened with demolition to allow for the widening of Sandy Lane in 1968; but it was saved and a year later it was decided to set back the boundary of the Manor House garden on the other side of the road to the north. One can still see today the remnant stub of the original boundary wall of the Manor House, seen on the left of this photo and now the extremity of the pavement on Sandy Lane.

The Manor House was originally built in the time of Queen Anne and was the home for a time of the famous architect Sir George Gilbert Scott, who lived here in the latter half of the 19th century.

The no. 71 bus route was diverted from its original route via Ham Common and Lock Road along Sandy Lane in about 1967 once the lane had been widened.

In this photo, the walls on both sides of the road are painted with white stripes. They were possibly added a few years earlier during the Second World War to assist sight of potential hazards during the blackouts. Sometimes posts, trees and even cows were also painted with these stripes!

HAM MANOR FARM AND SECRETT'S DAIRY

A photo taken in 1952 of the original Ham Manor Farm on the west side of Ham Street opposite what is now Grey Court School. At this time it was known as Secrett's Farm and Dairy after its tenant farmer. The house in the background faced an open courtyard with farm buildings (in the foreground of the photo, opposite), which included a dairy. Earlier, from about 1842, the farmer William Hatch took on the lease from the Dysarts and for 40 years, he cultivated mixed arable, pasture and meadow on Dysart land and the Lammas Lands, or the Common Fields (now known as Ham Lands).

Ham Close currently occupies the fields nearest to the farm and Ham Library is now on the site of Hatch's orchards. By 1881 his farm consisted of 430 acres, which was almost a quarter of the total area of Ham. The painting above of the farm dates from 1887. He employed twenty-one men, ten women and six boys. William married Jane, the daughter of

the Ham maltster, Daniel Light. He also farmed for a time at her family's Home Farm, which was at the other end of Ham Street behind the Malthouse. When he died in 1885 William's two youngest sons Henry and Daniel took over the farm but at the turn of the century the Earl of Dysart wanted to increase his return on the land and he reduced the area for arable farming in favour of the more profitable gravel extraction and market garden produce (vegetables and flowers). When Robert and John Ward took on the lease for a time in the early 1900s the farm amounted to only 170 acres. It was then leased to Archibald Secrett in 1918.

Archibald William Secrett was the son of a successful builder, Frederick Elijah Betts Secrett from Ealing in West London and younger brother of Frederick Augustus Secrett, known as 'F.A.', who was a pioneer vegetable grower during the Second World War. In 1915 Frederick took over the tenancy of Marsh Farm in Twickenham where he produced not only vegetables but daffodils and tulips, which he sold at Covent Garden Market in London. In 1937 he purchased Hurst Farm in Milford in Surrey, the now famous Secrett's Farm which is still run today by the same family. It became renowned as one of the most productive farms during the Second World War. F.A.'s younger brother, Archibald, supplied milk to the village of Ham from the Manor Farm Dairy and his cows were a familiar sight strolling down Ham Street from the fields after milking. Archibald's younger brother, Lewis Betts, known locally as 'Lou', took over from him in 1929 and ran the farm during the Second World War, by which time it only amounted to about 70 acres. Lou eventually sold most of his cattle, and the farm house and dairy on Ham Street, as seen in this photo, was pulled down in 1958. It is now the L-shape site of the shops at the corner of Ham Street and Ashburnham Road.

SECRETT'S COWS OUTSIDE HAM HOUSE STABLES

When Secrett's farmhouses were being demolished in June 1958 for housing development, an ancient structure was found in one of the buildings. Under the brick and stucco there was a timber structure with a 3-bay hall that had gothic windows, leaded lights and one-foot square oak beams. The walls were revealed to have been plastered with reeds, cow manure and sand dating from the reign of Elizabeth I, thus predating Ham House by almost 200 years. The drawing, right, by John Sanderson-Wells c.1940, shows the interior of the tithe barn before it was demolished.

The daily ritual of cows being herded from Secrett's Dairy was sometimes varied for them to graze in the field on the south side of Ham House, and they were then seen walking along the (then) narrow, Sandy Lane, (see page 38). Another drawing by John Sanderson-Wells from the same period shows the dairy cows outside the stables of Ham House on Ham Street, walking down Ham Street towards the river.

HAM LANDS

Eric Parker's charming book, *Highways and Byways in Surrey* was first written in 1908 when he walked through the country villages and towns of Surrey exploring and recording what he found. The following quote is taken from Chapter XXI, page 235, second edition, published some thirty years later in 1935:

When I first saw Ham, in the early years of this century, I walked out from Kingston to find myself suddenly in the fruitful spaces of market gardens and farms. It is the suddenest change. Kingston, with the oldest memories of all Surrey towns, was even then as new and noisy as a thoroughly efficient service of tramways could make it; and there, within a stone's throw of bricks and barracks, I came upon acres beyond acres of level farmland, bean-fields and cabbage-fields and all the pleasantness of tilled soil and trenched earth and the wealth of kindly fruits. When I saw the fields by Ham on that hot day in August there were country women gathering runner beans into coarse aprons, stooping over the clustered plants, the humblest and hardiest of workers of the farm. Under that hot sun, in the wide spaces of those unfenced fields, with no English hedge to shut off neighbouring crops and tillage, the air of those bent, lowly figures was of French peasantry, French nearness to the difficult livelihood of the soil. They might have gleaned for Millet; to cease their work at the Angelus. [This refers to Jean-François Millet's 1859 painting of the Angelus, depicting the rural scene of two peasants in a field who are bowing to pray over a basket of potatoes at the ringing of the church bell to mark the end of the day's work]. *That was many years ago. Today there are still patches of market garden between Ham and Kingston, but the peace of those fields has yielded to villa and road.*

This photo, c.1930, shows agricultural labourers working in the fields at harvest time. They are taking a break from loading hay onto a wagon. The hay has been cut by sickle and scythe and then dried in the field beforehand. It was exhausting work and had to be done quickly if the weather threatened to turn as it was important that the hay be kept dry prior to storing.

LOCK ROAD

Facing east towards Ham Common, the road followed the line of the old field path. Partially built in the 1890s the road ran from the Common as far as Craig Road, with farm land and flax fields beyond to Teddington Lock. The road was gradually extended to the west, reaching its current length in 1934, when it met Broughton Avenue.

The Malthouse at the end of Lock Road (see page 16) and shown in the middle of this photo was partially demolished in 1906, to allow Lock Road to widen and run straight to the Common. Hitherto the road joined with Back Lane and went around the buildings to the south, including the Malthouse Cottage, and came out onto the Common by the side of Ensleigh Lodge, as a very narrow lane.

This early 1900s photo shows John Whiting, in the white shirt, who lived in Evelyn Road (see page 23). He is seen turning into Craig Road where he worked as an agricultural labourer in the fields. The taller house on the right (now no. 34) was hit by a high explosive bomb in November 1940, in the Second World War. Although there was extensive damage, fortunately there were no casualties. The site, which now includes nos. 28, 30 and 32, was compulsorily purchased by the Richmond Borough Council and rebuilt after the War.

No. 45 Lock Road, opposite Craig Road, and behind the line of trees on the left-hand side of the photo, was rebuilt after the War. Built originally as a detached house in c.1897, it was specially constructed for the Violet Home for Crippled Children (see page 32). Later known as Hermiston, it became the home of William Harry Harland from 1902-1910. Known as 'the champion of Ham', he was a journalist who fought in 1891, along with other Ham villagers, for the rights of the commoners against the Lords of the Manor, the Dysarts (see page 23). He was well-educated and articulate and wrote *Ham Common and the Dysarts: A Brief and an Indictment* in 1894, a treatise which set out the rights of commoners when Charles I granted rights over the Common in return for the enclosure of Richmond Park. Harland set up the Ham Common Defence Committee to support the legal defence of the villagers accused of trespass.

It was Harland who named his home on Lock Road 'Hermiston' (thought to be taken from the novel by Robert Louis Stevenson, left unfinished by his sudden death in 1894). It was a name that he took with him to his next house, when he moved to East Horsley, where he died in 1932.

NEW ROAD

As with many streets in Ham today, New Road is lined with parked cars; this early 1900 photo has an eerie and uncanny feel to it without them. At the end of the road, one can see the rear of the Little House, which faces Ham Common.

On the extreme right was Gordon Hall, a corrugated iron building, where Violet Cavendish-Bentinck (see page 33) held Young Men's Bible Classes and lectures (see right). It was demolished in 1922 and replaced with new houses, now nos. 43, 45 and 47. The houses suffered war damage, as did Lock Road, in November 1940, and a Warden's Hut was erected for a time on the site during the War.

Sir George Gilbert Scott, the renowned architect, who lived at the Manor House, bought land to build the Working Men's Institute (half way down the road on the left, now no. 28), which was formed in 1869 for 'the amusement and instruction of the working men of the village'. Funds were raised for the building by public subscription and it was opened in November 1874 with Scott as its president. The hours were from 6pm until 10pm, except Sundays. Prior to this, meetings were held at the Dysart Coffee House, now no. 11 Ham Street, known as the Old Bakery. The Institute has now (2017) moved to the Royal Oak public house (see page 37) on Ham Street as the new Ham Village Centre, and the building on New Road has been converted into a large residential house.

The photo, right, of the Ham Institute shows the original porch of the Institute. It was probably taken at the opening of the new second storey which was built in 1905 to enlarge the building. Above right, is a notice in the St Andrew's Church parish magazine of 1897.

LECTURES ON HEALTH.

Three practical lectures to men only will be given in the Gordon Hall, by the kind invitation of Miss Cavendish Bentinck, on Wednesdays, 8th, 15th and 22nd December, at 7.30 p.m., by A. P. Schofield, Esq., M.D., etc., member of the Council of, and examiner to, the National Health Society, etc. The chair will be taken by James Walker, Esq.

SUBJECTS:

8th December.—How to avoid dying before our time.

15th December.—How to take care of number one.

22nd December.—What to eat and what to drink.

Miss Bentinck is kindly providing tea and coffee either at the beginning or close of the Lecture. Lads under 16 will not be admitted.

PREFABRICATED HOUSING

The 'prefabs', as they were known, were built by the Government's Temporary Housing Programme initiated by Sir Winston Churchill in 1943 to address the chronic housing shortage of the many thousands who had lost their homes in the blitz on London in the Second World War. Some 113 prefabs were built on the farm land and fields that had been to the rear of Manor Farm (see page 41). They stretched from Ashburnham Road in the south to Woodville Road in the north and went as far as Sheridan and Stuart Roads, and were known as 'The Close', later 'Ham Close'.

The photo, above right, dated 1952, shows the east-west main walkway towards Back Lane. The prefabs on the left are facing Woodville Road and their back gardens backed onto the walkway. The bungalows had central heating and for some it was the first time they had the use of running hot water and an inside flushing toilet. Constructed with pre-cast reinforced concrete panels and roofs, they were pre-decorated in an off-white colour with gloss-green doors and trimmings.

In 1960 it was suggested that the prefabs be replaced with 9-storey blocks of flats. But eventually the development that was to be called Ham Close was reduced to 5-, 4- and 3-storey blocks, which were completed by 1963. Some of the prefabs had to be vacated and then demolished before the building of the flats could start and families had to be accommodated temporarily before they were permanently rehoused. The Ham Close flats provided homes for 192 families and cost about £500,000 to build. Rents ranged from £2 and 3s a week for a bed-sit to £4 for a three-bed-roomed maisonette. There was also a weekly charge ranging from 15s 6p to £1 for the supply of gas for central heating and cooking.

The photo opposite shows, on the right, some of the prefabs that faced Woodville Road. The council houses on the left were built before the Second World War and were larger than most in Ham, having four bedrooms. They originally housed larger families, of which there were many in Ham at the time. For example, at the end of the row, on the extreme right, no. 2 was the home of Harry and Kathleen 'Kitty' Morris, who had 13 children; next to them at no. 4, the family of Fred and Edith Wills, who had in total 18 children; then Bill and Kitty Nutbeam at no. 6, with 11 children; and at no. 8 the Alfred Smith family, with 11 children. It was a very close-knit community, with the families mixing and socialising together; and there were a number of marriages between the families. At that time, there were few cars and local kids were often at play outside on the roads, which you don't see today.

In February 1994, the Daily Mail ran a feature about large working class families and how they managed to cope in the post-war days. It featured the Wills family from Ham. A quote from that paper is particularly poignant; 'A paper round at five, socks from old sleeves, and eight to a bed, but still such happy days'.

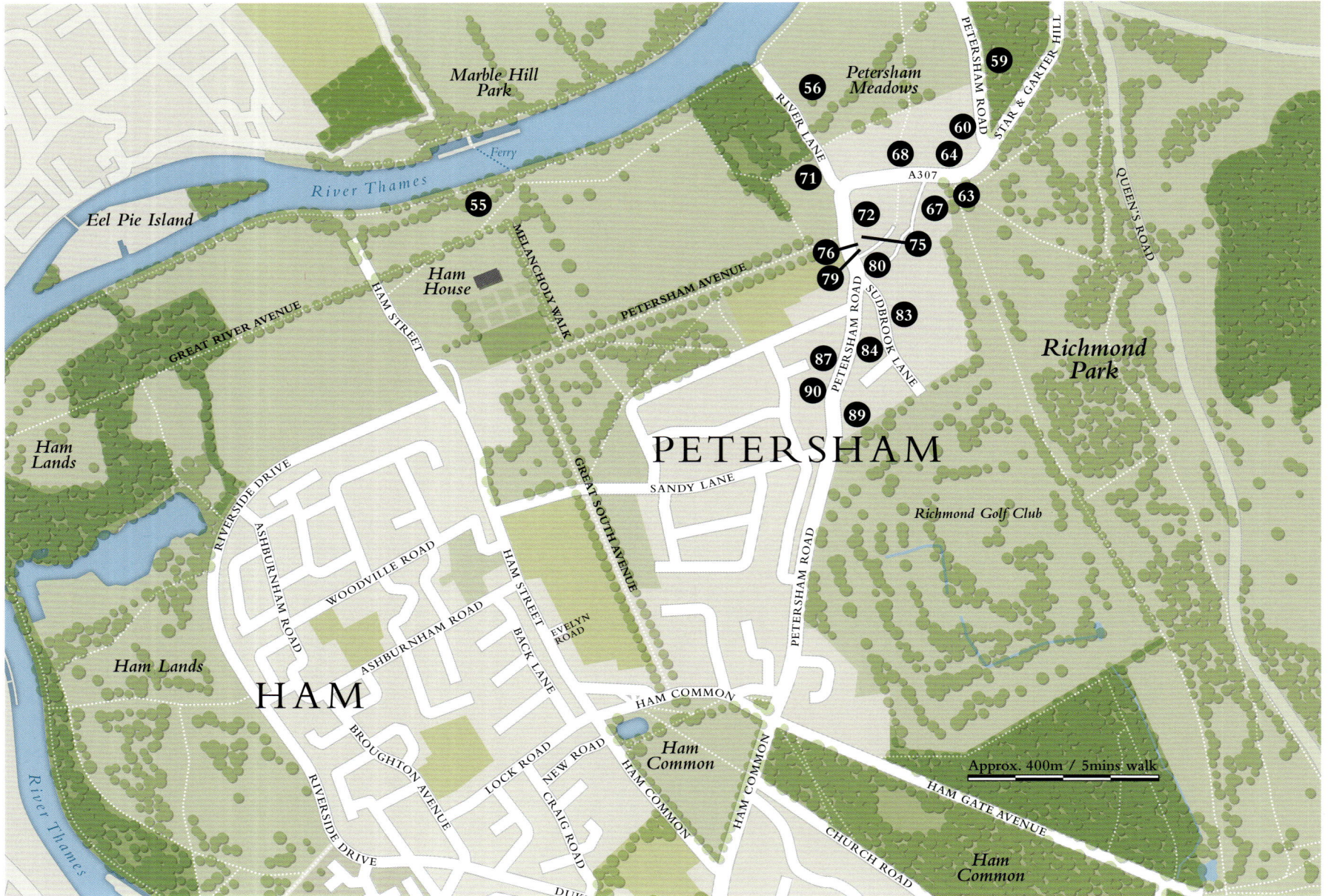

Marble Hill Park

Petersham Meadows

PETERSHAM ROAD

STAR & GARTER HILL

RIVER LANE

59

56

60

68 **64**

71

A307

55

River Thames

Eel Pie Island

72

67 **63**

76 **75**

79 **80**

Ham House

MELANCHOLY WALK

PETERSHAM AVENUE

83

GREAT RIVER AVENUE

PETERSHAM ROAD

SUDBROOK LANE

84

QUEEN'S ROAD

Richmond Park

87

90

89

Ham Lands

Richmond Golf Club

PETERSHAM

HAM STREET

GREAT SOUTH AVENUE

Sandy Lane

RIVERSIDE DRIVE

ASHBURNHAM ROAD

WOODVILLE ROAD

ASHBURNHAM ROAD

HAM STREET

BACK LANE

EVELYN ROAD

PETERSHAM ROAD

Ham Lands

HAM

BROUGHTON AVENUE

RIVERSIDE DRIVE

LOCK ROAD

NEW ROAD

CRAIG ROAD

HAM COMMON

Ham Common

HAM COMMON

HAM COMMON

HAM COMMON

CHURCH ROAD

HAM GATE AVENUE

Ham Common

Approx. 400m / 5mins walk

DUKE

River Thames

Ferry

Key to Map for Petersham

The page numbers of each page given above are also shown on the map opposite

THE RIVER THAMES

The postcard opposite shows a common sight in the early 1900s alongside the river at Ham, where the Ham Street car park is today, upstream from Petersham and Richmond. This landscape has been the backdrop to the famous and world-renowned view from Richmond Hill so often depicted in paintings. There are rich floodplains alongside the river which provided good pastureland for dairy cows, which used to graze freely on these meadows until well into the 1950s.

Over the years, the Dysart family of Ham House had greatly influenced the historic development of the Ham and Petersham area. Originally most of it was Royal Manorial land, leased to the earls of Dysart. Over the years they acquired the freehold and sub-leased to tenant farmers. Ham, particularly, was an agricultural community; it wasn't until the 1930s that major housing developments took place here.

Ever since 1672, the Dysarts had claimed ownership over the towpath or barge way, from Richmond to Teddington, charging 3d for each horse, with toll houses at the end of River Lane and opposite Eel Pie Island.

The towing path, or 'Silent Highway' as it was known, was on the Surrey bank, and horses plied up and down, towing barges with goods and merchandise from London via Richmond upriver towards Kingston Bridge.

Until the 19th century, some of the towing horses used on this stretch of the river were kept at stables at what is now the Forge Garage on the Petersham Road (see page 74), where there was also a smithy and farrier. Many of the watermen who worked on the river lived in Petersham.

Sir Walter Scott describes this view in *The Heart of Midlothian*, his novel written in 1818:

'A huge sea of verdure with crossing and interesting promontories of massive and tufted groves......tenanted by numberless flocks and herds, which seem to wander unrestrained, and unbounded, through rich pastures. The Thames, here turreted with villas and there garlanded with forests, moved on slowly and placidly, like the mighty monarch of the scene, to whom all its other beauties were accessories, and bore on his bosom a hundred barks and skiffs, whose white sails and gaily fluttering pennons gave life to the whole.'

PETERSHAM MEADOWS

The horse that pulled the F & H E Hornby milk delivery wagon in this 1900s photo was apparently known as 'White Face'. The grazing cattle in the background have always been very much part of the famous view from Richmond Hill. In the far distance on the right can be seen The Star and Garter Hotel, the original building that was designed by E M Barry. The Petersham Hotel that used to be known as both the Mansion Hotel and the Star and Garter before 1978, is in the middle background, just off Nightingale Lane.

William Wordsworth mentions the nightingales for which Richmond Hill was once famous in a sonnet he wrote in June 1820:

'Fame tells of groves – from England far away –
Groves that inspire the Nightingale to trill
And modulate, with subtle reach of skill
Elsewhere unmatched, her ever-varying lay;
Such bold report I venture to gainsay:
For I have heard the quire of Richmond Hill
Chanting, with indefatigable bill,
Strains that recalled to mind a distant day'

In 1870 the two brothers, Frederick and Henry Epton Hornby, leased the meadows together with the farm at River Lane, which amounted to about 30 acres. They were both dairy farmers and it was Henry who started a model dairy farm at Petersham and built up a chain of dairy shops in the district, selling their produce under the name of F & H E Hornby. According to an advertisement in the 1900 edition of the Kelly's Directory, they sold milk at that time for 4d a quart.

In 1917 the business was amalgamated with J. Clarke & Sons, after the death of Josiah Clarke, who ran a rival local dairy business. As Hornby & Clarke Ltd they had their own herd of pedigree Guernsey cows that produced a particular quality of rich milk. They were milked by machine and there was a cooling and bottling plant at the model dairy, London's only dairy farm at that time. The horse-drawn wagons were gradually replaced with mechanised trucks. Their head office was in Princes Street in Richmond, and as well as supplying milk from Petersham and other farms they also had sixteen branch shops selling dairy products and groceries. By 1960 they were having difficulties maintaining the farm as a going concern and they sold out to Express Dairy Co. Ltd. Milk production continued on the meadows until the 1980s.

In 1990 Chris Brasher, the former athletics champion who lived in River Lane, founded the Petersham Trust, which was set up to protect, conserve, maintain and enhance the meadows for the benefit of the general public and to maintain a herd of grazing cattle on the meadows. The Trust eventually raised sufficient money for an endowment fund that enabled the National Trust to assume responsibility for the meadows.

PETERSHAM ALMSHOUSES

The first almshouses on Petersham Common (see page 61) were built in 1729 on the north-west extremity of the Common. Apparently, the owner of Wick House on Richmond Hill complained about the smell of pigs kept by the occupants and in 1809, they were relocated to the bottom of the hill on a new site which fronted the road to Richmond, now the Petersham Road, close to the Rose of York public house.

By the mid-1800s they were in a state of disrepair and it was decided to rebuild them. This was made possible by an endowment from Madame Tildesley de Bosset, an heiress and widow from Belgium who apparently often visited the Star and Garter Hotel. She died in 1867 and in her will she bequeathed to the parish of Petersham a total of £3,800 for the building and endowment of the new almshouses. Her wishes were that every inmate should be a member of the Church of England; be aged not less than 50 years old; of honest and sober life; and to have resided not less than three years in the parish of Petersham. The new almshouses consisted of five tenements; the central one had an upper and lower floor. The photo on the right with the large Star and Garter Hotel behind it was taken c. 1875.

This is a copy of the 1867 rules (from the report of the Charity Commissioners of 1894) that was to be hung in each house, 'in some conspicuous place, and each Inmate before admission shall sign a copy of such Rules, and an Agreement to vacate the house, on being so required by the Trustees, for breach of any rule'.

Generally, the occupants were women, although there were some male inmates in the early part of 1891. Each tenement consisted of a sitting-room with a dark and not very convenient bedroom attached. At the time of the 1894 Charity Commissioner's report, the residents were each given an allowance of 5s a week, which was supplemented

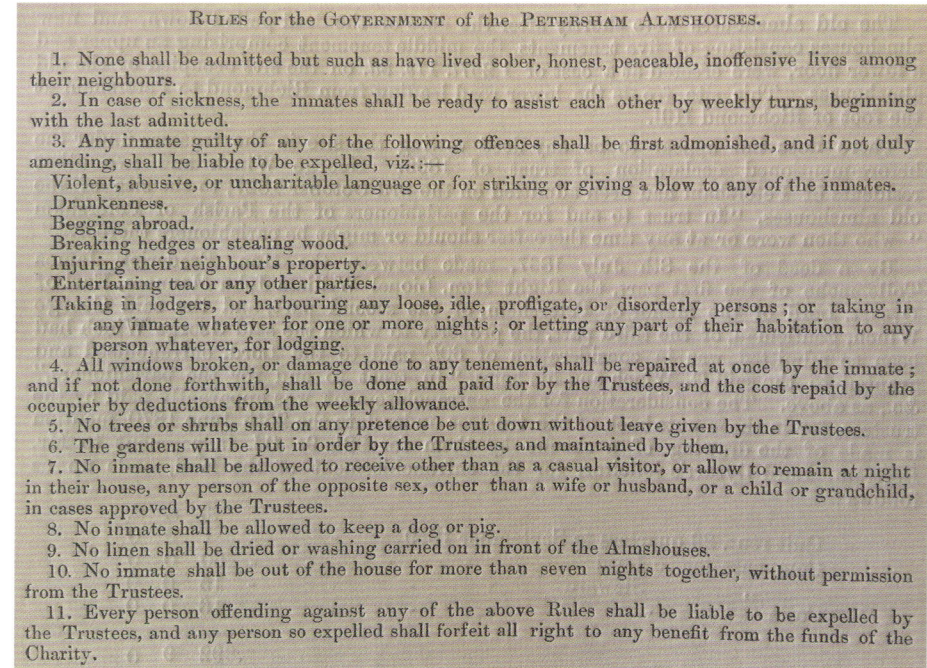

RULES for the GOVERNMENT of the PETERSHAM ALMSHOUSES.

1. None shall be admitted but such as have lived sober, honest, peaceable, inoffensive lives among their neighbours.

2. In case of sickness, the inmates shall be ready to assist each other by weekly turns, beginning with the last admitted.

3. Any inmate guilty of any of the following offences shall be first admonished, and if not duly amending, shall be liable to be expelled, viz.:—

Violent, abusive, or uncharitable language or for striking or giving a blow to any of the inmates.
Drunkenness.
Begging abroad.
Breaking hedges or stealing wood.
Injuring their neighbour's property.
Entertaining tea or any other parties.
Taking in lodgers, or harbouring any loose, idle, profligate, or disorderly persons; or taking in any inmate whatever for one or more nights; or letting any part of their habitation to any person whatever, for lodging.

4. All windows broken, or damage done to any tenement, shall be repaired at once by the inmate; and if not done forthwith, shall be done and paid for by the Trustees, and the cost repaid by the occupier by deductions from the weekly allowance.

5. No trees or shrubs shall on any pretence be cut down without leave given by the Trustees.

6. The gardens will be put in order by the Trustees, and maintained by them.

7. No inmate shall be allowed to receive other than as a casual visitor, or allow to remain at night in their house, any person of the opposite sex, other than a wife or husband, or a child or grandchild, in cases approved by the Trustees.

8. No inmate shall be allowed to keep a dog or pig.

9. No linen shall be dried or washing carried on in front of the Almshouses.

10. No inmate shall be out of the house for more than seven nights together, without permission from the Trustees.

11. Every person offending against any of the above Rules shall be liable to be expelled by the Trustees, and any person so expelled shall forfeit all right to any benefit from the funds of the Charity.

by groceries supplied by the parish.

By December 1952 the buildings were subsiding and in danger of collapse. They were also apparently very damp. The fact that the foundations were on clay did not help. By this time only two of the almshouses were occupied. Miss Emily Dixon aged 80 years, who had been hospitalised with a broken leg; and Mrs Agnes Appleton, aged 76, whose house in Petersham had been bombed in the Second World War. Initially they were reluctant to leave, but had done so by March 1953, when the demolition work started in May of that year.

Peterhsam Road and The Star and Garter Hill

A rural scene in Petersham in the early 1900s; the wooded area to the right of the photo is known as Petersham Common or the Petersham Woods, at the foot of the Star and Garter Hill. The broad-leaved woodland is an area of approximately 17.5 acres and because livestock could graze there, it used to be free of the dense undergrowth that is there now. It is bordered by the Star and Garter Hill on the south side; Richmond Hill on the east side; and the Petersham Road on the west side. The Common is now managed by the Petersham Common Conservators, who maintain the site. This dates from the 1902 Ham and Petersham Open Spaces Act of Parliament when the ownership of the Common by the Dysarts was made over to the Richmond Borough Council 'for public enjoyment'. The nine Conservators still manage the Common today and are made up of six individuals appointed by the local authority and three appointed by the Petersham parish vestry. They meet to manage the Common four times a year. Today the Common has a designation as a Site of Metropolitan Importance for Nature Conservation.

This photo shows the Petersham Road on the west side of the Common at the foot of the hill. It is the road that connects Petersham to Richmond further north. The original level of the road still exists as a path at the bottom of the hill along the border of Petersham Farm (once known as Star Farm) and Petersham meadows. The lower causeway (or 'the causey', as it was also known), is recorded in the Richmond Manor Court Rolls as far back as 1569. It used to flood regularly and because it was often impassable an alternative route was developed up Richmond Hill. The lower causeway was also moved higher up the hill and renamed the Petersham Road c.1893. In this photo the road still has a sandy surface. Later, in 1923, the road was widened to accommodate the increase in traffic.

In 1899 forty competitors took part in motor-vehicle hill-climbing trials organised by the Automobile Club of Great Britain on the Star and Garter Hill. One of them was the Hon Charles Stewart Rolls who, with Sir Frederick Henry Royce, went on, in 1904, to found the Rolls-Royce British luxury-car and aircraft-engine manufacturing business. Apparently the most exciting part of the event was the descent after the finish, when speeds were too much for the vehicles' braking capabilities.

THE OLD RUSSELL SCHOOL

Although there were some small fee-paying schools for the better-off, situated in one or two larger houses in Petersham, prior to 1850 there was only a small infant's parochial school in a small corrugated-iron building on Sandpits Lane, later renamed Sandpits Road. For many years the same building was also used as a Sunday School. This changed at the behest of Lord John Russell, 1st Earl Russell, who had leased Pembroke Lodge in Richmond Park. Russell was the principal architect of the Great Reform Act of 1832, and went on to become a Whig Prime Minister twice. Lord and Lady Russell gave £1,500 as an endowment to build a new school in 1849, and three years later this purpose-built school, together with a master's house, was constructed inside the walls of Richmond Park close to Petersham Gate. The countess noted in her diary that year, 'Our little school, which had long been planned, was opened in a room in the village the day before Baby's birthday, July 10 and goes on well. We celebrated John's birthday [their son, John Russell, Viscount Amberley, was 10 years old] last Saturday by giving the school children a tea under the cedar and a dance on the lawn afterwards and very merry they were'. Lord Russell believed in civil and religious liberty, and from the beginning the school was closely associated with the British Society, who established non-denominational schools 'for children of the poorer classes'. At the time there was some opposition from the largely Anglican community in Petersham to this new radical approach to schooling. However, it became known as the Russell British School, starting with just 12 boys and 12 girls, and was to flourish. School attendance, if available at all, was voluntary until 1870 when the landmark Education Act was passed, which provided free national elementary education.

The school was subsequently enlarged in 1875, at a time when the total population of Petersham was about 683, to accommodate infants. The master Ebeneezer Wilkes Smith and his wife who worked at the school for 24 years were particular favourites of Lady Russell. It remained under the patronage of the Russell family until 1891, when it was fully transferred to the authority of the British and Foreign Schools Society. The children at that time went on to be apprentices in trades and became plumbers, bakers, tailors and dressmakers. Many also went into service mainly to the large houses in the area. In 1903, about the time the photo, left, of the school was taken, the Richmond Borough Council Education Committee minutes show an attendance of 41 boys, 31 girls and 20 infants; 9 of the infants were under five years old. For almost 100 years this was the location of the local village school for Petersham.

The photo opposite shows the children at play with their teacher in the 1920s under a large London Plane tree in the grounds of Richmond Park, looking down towards the Petersham Road. The rear of the school is behind them. Years before, this area had been part of the grounds of the Old Petersham Lodge, a fine mansion that had origins that dated back to the 17th century and housed the Cole family, Lords of the Manor before the Dysarts.

The school was badly damaged by a Second World War bomb in November 1943 and the building had to be pulled down. The site then reverted to parkland. In 1954 the school moved to its present location on the Petersham Road, opposite the Fox and Duck public house. The Orchard Junior School had opened there in 1952 and the two amalgamated as the Russell School in 1980.

THE DYSART ARMS

This public house and local landmark is situated at the bottom of the steep Star and Garter Hill, opposite the Petersham pedestrian entrance to Richmond Park. There has been an inn on this site since the early 17th century; prior to that it was a farmhouse. Its first known name was the Plough and Harrow. The name was changed to the Dysart Arms in the 1830s. It has been said that Louisa, the 7th Countess of Dysart, paid for the name to be changed. As can be seen from the sign on the extreme left, the proprietor in the early 1900s was Samuel Vine. He was the landlord for many years and, according the Richmond Herald of 1902, Chairman of the Licensed Victuallers Protection Society! Notice the front door of the inn, which had a wooden-trellised entrance, a feature of many houses in Petersham that can still be found today. The Dysart coat of arms and a magnificent lamp hung above the front entrance. The building was pulled down in 1902 and replaced with the present Dysart Arms, with its exposed oak beams and plaster work, which was designed by the influential Suffolk architect John Shewell Corder.

Every year on Ascension Day, until the early 1850s, when detailed Ordnance Survey maps were introduced on a larger scale, 'Beating the Bounds' started from the Inn. The ceremony was an ancient tradition that delineated the parish boundary to ensure that it was not forgotten. It has been recorded that whenever a boundary mark was found the nearest boy was seized and his head was banged against the stone – just so that he would remember! Dinner at 3s 6d a head followed at the inn, and no doubt a beer or two. It was thirsty work!

BUTE HOUSE

Next door to the Petersham Gate (the western entrance to Richmond Park on the Petersham Road), there used to be a grand mansion called Bute House, set within a very large estate. This photo, taken just prior to its demolition, shows the front of the house, which faced south towards the Park and some of its extensive grounds. There were kitchen gardens, orchards, a conservatory, lawns and shrubbery walks shaded by fine cedars, all screened from the road by a high wall. The house took its name from John Stuart, 1st Marquess of Bute, who inherited the property from his uncle in 1796. He had married, as his second wife, Frances or 'Fanny', the youngest daughter of the banker Thomas Coutts, and it is thought that it was her family who funded major alterations to the house in about 1805. The property remained in the family for almost 100 years.

A subterraneous passage linked the house to Church House on the opposite side of the Petersham Road. For twenty-five years, Church House was the home of Paul Amedée Francis Coutts-Stuart, the grandson of the 1st Marquess. As a result of a riding accident, he had sustained brain damage and was cared for here until his death in 1883, aged 63. The house was separated from the estate and sold in 1889.

The passage was used as a trench shelter in the Second World War and could accommodate 47 people and had 24 bunks. Trench shelters were used to accommodate people who did not have their own gardens where they could install their own smaller Anderson shelters, named after Sir John Anderson, the man responsible for preparing Britain to withstand Nazi air raids. The passage existed until it was eventually bricked up in the 1980s.

Bute House had ceased to be a residential home by 1870, and had become a school 'for the sons of gentlemen', which was run by the Revd. Charles Vincent Godby, with 80 boarding pupils. The figures in this photo may well be some of the school boys.

The estate was acquired by Sir John Whittaker Ellis in 1889, just after this photo was taken. Born at the old Star and Garter Hotel, Whittaker Ellis was Lord Mayor of London in 1881 and a few years later, the first Mayor of Richmond. He summarily demolished the house in 1895 and intended to sell the land for the development of 30 houses. There were letters in the Times to avert this 'Villadom' of Petersham, and attempts were made to merge the fine grounds with the Park. Depositions were made in May 1895 to the Government by the Commons Preservation Society, the Richmond Borough Council, the Metropolitan Public Gardens Association and others demanding that they step in with the required £8,500 to preserve this historic landscape. The National Trust also lent its support to the appeal. All to no avail. However, three years later the estate was saved, bought by Lætitia Rachael Warde, who was the widow of Henry Lionel Warde and daughter of Samuel Walker of Petersham House. Her father had died in April 1898 and left her a substantial fortune.

Mrs Warde built All Saints' Church on the south-east end of the Bute House Estate as a memorial to her parents. She died in 1906 and it was her son Lionel who completed the building in 1909. It was many years later that the rest of the Estate was developed for housing. In the 1930s, Bute Avenue, which led from Sudbrook Lane to the new Church was built. Later in the 1960s, Cedar Heights and Ashfield Close (named after Marjorie Ashfield, Lionel's daughter) were built.

ST PETER'S CHURCH

This early watercolour was painted from the north side of St Peter's Church, with Petersham House behind the tree and the wall on the right. The artist is not known, but the painting bears a striking resemblance to others painted at the time (c.1820) by Lady Caroline Scott, the wife of Vice Admiral Sir George Scott, who lived at Douglas House.

Sir Nikolaus Pevsner described St Peter's as 'of uncommon charm', with elements that date back to medieval times. The notable cupola dates from c.1720, when it replaced a spire. Much of fabric of the church seen in this painting dates from the early 1500s and still exists today. It retains a remarkable pre-Victorian interior with a full set of fine box pews and galleries. When the Revd. Richard Sawbridge Mills arrived here at the living in 1929, the church was still lit by gas.

The churchyard was extended to the east in 1801, taking in part of the kitchen garden at the rear of Parkgate, and again in 1863, when a small strip of land to the north, from what was known as Walnut Tree field, was purchased from the 8th Earl of Dysart. It was further enlarged in 1919 at the behest of the banker George Tournay Biddulph, who also lived at Douglas House from 1906-1929. He purchased another strip of the Walnut Tree field from the Dysarts for the Church.

Petersham's long history as an aristocratic and suburban retreat is evidenced by those that lie buried in the churchyard. Along with humble parishioners there are many noblemen, including many from the Dysart family, as well as eminent literary and national celebrities, distinguished soldiers and sailors, and most notably the navigator and explorer Captain George Vancouver, who lived at Glen Cottage on River Lane (see page 72).

In his *Lines on the View from Petersham Hill* the Revd. William Henry Oxley, vicar of St Peter's 1891-1913 (see page 84) wrote about the churchyard:

'Here courtiers, statesmen, cavaliers,
The Penns, Vancouver, Berrys, peers
And peasants, long since dead
With Indians from some far-off shore,
Proud Lauderdale, and many more
Rest in their quiet bed'

The poem refers to the Penn family, descendants of William Penn, who was the founder of Pennsylvania; George Vancouver (see page 70); Mary Berry, the authoress and her sister Agnes, friends of Horace Walpole; and some of the Dysart and Lauderdale family, who were buried at St Peter's.

GLEN COTTAGE, RIVER LANE

Little is known about the history of Glen Cottage and the Navigator's House, which is attached to it, on River Lane. The drawing opposite was made by Edward Walker in about 1940 for the *Recording Britain Collection*. The origins of the houses are several hundred years old, although the Navigator's House has been completely re-built. There is a record in the Manor Court Rolls dated May 1675 that probably refers to the pair of cottages as 'two messuages and an orchard'.

Captain George Vancouver, the great Pacific coast explorer, surveyor and navigator, spent the last two years of his life here. He died, aged 40, in 1798. It is where he is said to have written *Voyage of Discovery to the North Pacific and around the World*. Vancouver rose from being a seaman under Captain Cook in the Royal Navy to command the ship Discovery, which made a voyage of exploration in 1791-95 in the Pacific and along the western seaboard of North America, which he was the first to delineate accurately. He circumnavigated the island which now bears his name. He is buried at St Peter's and every year, in May, a commemorative service is held at his grave.

The Navigator's House was previously known as Craigmyle (seen on the right-hand side of the drawing). This was the home for a time of Charles G Harper (1863-1943). An artist and author, from 1892 he travelled all over England on a bicycle with nothing but 'a razor and a piece of comb', as well as sketching materials for his travel books and his notebooks and pencils. He engaged and talked to country people wherever he went, recording many literary landmarks as well as the old highways and the coaches that travelled on them. *Rural Nooks round London* (see page 74), was published in 1907. He lived at Craigmyle towards the end of his life with his wife and elderly blind mother before moving to a house in Hazel Lane then called 'Rookwood'. He died aged 80 and was also buried at St Peter's.

Farm lodge, Petersham Road

It has been claimed that the mid-18th century Avenue and Farm Lodges on the Petersham Road were a pair of early cottages that marked the entrance to the Old Petersham Lodge in Richmond Park (demolished in 1835). It is now thought that they most probably flanked the stable yard of Montrose House.

These photos show the lodge to the north, Farm Lodge. It shows Rachel Colborne at her front door, surrounded by honeysuckle, and was taken by a Mr Hopkins in April 1901. Rachel, née Dobbs, had married Arthur Colborne, a widower in 1864. He was a local carpenter and journeyman and had lived at Farm Lodge for over 40 years. Shortly after Arthur died in 1902, his wife Rachel ran the Richmond Free Library branch reading-room at Petersham, on the ground floor room of the Lodge which fronted the Petersham Road, to the left of where she is standing at her front door. She was paid one guinea a month for her services by the Richmond Borough Council. The reading room closed in August 1908 as the cost was not considered justified by the average daily attendance of only 1.7 people, this despite a representation to the Richmond Library Committee on behalf of the Petersham parish vestry by two notable parishioners, John Henry Master JP, of Montrose House, and George Tournay Biddulph, of Douglas House.

FORGE GARAGE, PETERSHAM ROAD

The collection of out-buildings in this photo was at the rear of Farm Lodge and Avenue Lodge on the Petersham Road. The photo, taken from *Rural Nooks round London* by Charles G. Harper (see page 70) in c.1907, is described as the Blacksmith's shop. Land tax returns in 1780 show that they were owned, as were so many properties in Petersham, by the Dysarts. Farm Lodge had stables attached to the house at the rear which were used by river bargemen and watermen for their towing horses. Apparently up to 70 horses could be stabled here overnight. Next to the stables there was also a smithy shop with a farrier.

James Veal was the blacksmith at the shop in 1800. Henry Winch, who lived at Farm Lodge prior to Arthur Colborne (see page 73) was a coal merchant as well as a farrier and general smith (1870-1890). His father had been a barge horse master. In 1870, Benjamin Lovett was the farrier and blacksmith. In 1881, the Census records that Harry Beard was manufacturing bicycles in the yard and by 1895 commercial directories show that Walter Fish was the local shoeing smith. Shortly after this photo was taken, automobile and coach building repairs replaced the blacksmith and farrier.

By 1913 the yard was being used by the Richmond Borough Council as a storage depot and after the First World War it became a motor garage with a workshop and a small petrol station at the front. It became known as The Forge Garage. In 2006 the yard area was converted into residential mews houses.

FOX AND DUCK PUBLIC HOUSE — 1

Once a coaching inn and posting house on the stagecoach route from London, the Fox and Duck public house and hotel dates from the early 1700s. One of the last timber-structured inns in the district, it was demolished in 1940, along with the cottages seen in this 1905 photo. The two-storey public house that we see today replaced it, set further back from the road and built in the mock Georgian style. Note the precarious external chimney stack joined to the left of the Hotel. Also on the left of the photo one can just see a single-storey, white-boarded, slate-roofed building, which is the original village watchman's hut and lock-up (see page 78).

When the new Fox and Duck was rebuilt in 1940, the lock-up, still intact, was moved back to just in front of the archway of the Forge Garage. There was a pound area at the back of the lock-up that was used as a holding area for stray cattle until they were claimed by their owners. There is a mention in the St Peter's parish records of the pound existing together with wooden stocks even before the lock-up was built. Parish councils introduced lock-ups in the late 18th century to deal with the increase in vagrancy and drunkenness, and nearly every village in the country had its own lock-up. In particular, Petersham was seen as unsafe for travellers: the district being fairly wooded, it could be very dark. In 1772, during the reign of George III, the parish vestry was relieved of the responsibility for maintaining the highways and a body of trustees appointed for 'amending and keeping the said highways and roads in repair, and for causing the said roads to be lighted and watched in the night time'. An Act of Parliament was prepared by the Surveyor of the Highways for repairing and lighting the highways of the parish from Kingston to Richmond. It was paid for by rate payers at an annual charge 'not exceeding 1s 6d per £1'. The Petersham Highway Act was still in force in 1892, by which time the parish had been absorbed into the Borough of Richmond.

Fox and Duck Public House – 2

In this later photo of the Fox and Duck public house, taken from the other side of the Petersham Road, there is a clearer view, to the left of the building, of the village lock-up, which was erected in 1787. The parish constable or watchman was also known as Sergeant of the Night. The lock-up housed the watchman with his musket, bayonet, pair of pistols, cartridge box, 3 pounds of grapeshot, powder flask, lantern and his greatcoat, to keep him warm throughout the long winter nights. In 1787 the watchman was paid 11s a week to guard the village from 9 o'clock at night to 3 o'clock in the morning. He had orders from the parish vestry to 'stop all strangers of a suspicious appearance found in the parish, or conveying articles in carts or otherwise at unseasonable hours and not being able to give a good account of themselves'. In 1821 Richard Wigley of Ham was employed as a watchman. He attempted to stop a horse and cart driven by a Robert Knight of Richmond. Knight was engaged in smuggling spirits at the time. Wigley shot Knight in the head and he died shortly after. The affair excited a great deal of interest and was reported in the Times newspaper. Wigley was committed for murder and the case was heard at the Surrey Assizes at Kingston. Wigley was found guilty of manslaughter and sentenced to six months' imprisonment.

The Metropolitan Police was formed in 1829 and by the late 1830s the new police force had taken over most of the outer areas of London. As new police stations were built, lock-ups became redundant and most were pulled down for development as they were situated on prime sites in town centres. It is thought that the Petersham lock-up survived as the Richmond Borough Council used it as a storeroom for their tools. In 1955, the lock-up survived another reprieve. Some Petersham villagers felt that it should be demolished on account of its dilapidated state. Fortunately, the Ancient Monuments Committee stepped in and decided that it was worth preserving and repairs were undertaken. Since that time the lock-up is acknowledged to be a Monument at Risk and has a Grade II listed building status. It continues to be maintained by the Richmond Borough Council.

In the distance, on the right of the photo, is the 118ft tower of All Saints' Church on Bute Avenue, off Sudbrook Lane (see page 66). The church was designed by the architect John Kelly and built in the Romanesque style using red brick and terracotta tiles. It was surmounted by a bronze figure of Christ. In 1940 the church was requisitioned by the Army and used as a radar training school and the tower was used as a radar post. The church was never consecrated, it was used as a church occasionally, and was also used by the Greek Orthodox Church for a time. It became a recording studio until eventually, in the early 2000s, it was converted into a private house.

The buildings on the left of the photo formed part of the blacksmith's shop or the Forge Garage, as it became known. Between 1895 and 1907, on the extreme right and on the other side of the road to the Fox and Duck, where the current Russell School is now situated, Mrs Jane Gratwick ran the Fox and Duck tea gardens. Note the old water pump and early fire alarm system on the edge of the pavement opposite the lock-up.

PETERSHAM STORES, PETERSHAM ROAD

Myrtle Cottage, on the left of the Petersham Stores in the photo opposite, was built before the 1840s and was a lodging house for a time, run by Mrs Lydia Fruin. The single-storey grocery store, on the junction of Sudbrook Lane, was built on the south side of the cottage in the early 1880s. The shop thrived for many years until it was pulled down when Bute Cottages (now Bute Gardens) were built at the end of Sudbrook Lane, where it joins the Petersham Road, in 1906. This photo would have been taken just prior to its demolition. There is no evidence that there was ever a post office at this site, (although there was a post office next door in the 1920s, see page 82), despite there being two uniformed young men standing on the right of the stores. They are wearing the distinctive shako peaked hat worn by post men and telegram delivery boys of the time. The post men made on average four deliveries a day and they had a lot of walking to do around the village.

Another photo, below, c.1950 is of the Petersham Road, opposite the post office at Ivy Cottage. To the left of the road sweeper is no. 177, built c.1750; it is noticeable for its boarded façade, made from the bargeboards of boats from the river.

Butler's Posting Stables, Sudbrook Lane

This watercolour was painted in 1891 by the Revd. William Henry Oxley, who was appointed to the living of St Peter's, and was the vicar there for twenty-two years. He was a keen antiquarian and published some poems, including *Lines on the View from Petersham Hill*. The painting shows that he was also a talented painter. From the dilapidated state of the posting stables, the Revd. Oxley must have painted it shortly before its demolition in 1906 to make way for Bute Gardens (see page 81) previously Bute Cottages, on Sudbrook Lane that we see today.

William Butler lived at Box Cottage on Sudbrook Lane and was a fly- and carriage- proprietor in the latter half of the 19th century. It was a family business: as well as his father John before him, William and his two sons, William John and Francis, were fly- and carriage- and then omnibus drivers. William's posting stables were opposite the Petersham Arms, for a time known as the Sudbrook Arms, now Newark Lodge. In the 1880s, there were four cottages next door to the stables that were known as Butler's Cottages. The 1891 Census shows that William was still living at Box Cottage. He died a year later and is buried at St Peter's.

In 1922 John Keay & Son Ltd opened a grocery store at the corner shop at no. 6 Bute Gardens, formerly Bute Cottages on the junction of Sudbrook Lane and the Petersham Road. Keay's also had a branch in Richmond; the store at Petersham was managed for many years by Mr Gent. There was also a post office at the back of the store when the one at Ivy Cottage (see page 85) closed in 1924. The shop flourished for many years as the principal store in the area, closing in the late 1970s, after which time there was no longer a post office at Petersham. Keay's shop was converted into a residential house but is still known as the Post Office.

Ivy Cottage, Petersham Road

Ivy Cottage, no. 226 Petersham Road was for a time two separate dwellings. This 1907 photo shows the little wooden building to the north of the property was the original Petersham post office and for many years associated with the Long family. The earliest member mentioned in the church records of St Peter's is Francis Long, who married Ellen Cook in 1675; the family have featured in Petersham for several generations as dairymen, builders, undertakers and carpenters. The Land tax records show a shop and house for the first time in 1807, on land leased to John Long by the Dysarts. But it is possible that the Long family had associations with the Ivy Cottage site from earlier in the 18th century. John was a great-grandson of Francis and lived here and worked in the carpenter's shop, at the rear of the house, for many years. He was a craftsman who made the pulpit for St Peter's Church in 1796. He also ran a funeral business and made the wooden coffins. As time went on, a complex of buildings was added to the rear of the cottage; these were occupied by various tradesmen, including a tailor, David Williams, and a shoemaker, George Wallace.

In 1830, Henry Long, a builder and bricklayer, worked and lived here. In 1823 he had married a local girl, Lydia Maria Painter. She was the daughter of Thomas Painter, the parish Beadle. By the time of Henry's death in 1832, Lydia had established a grocery store in the one-storey, wooden building and ten years later, a small post office. Lydia became Petersham's first post-mistress. Hitherto there had only been a collecting box situated at the Fox and Duck public house. In the 1860s John Long's nephew Thomas, who was the son of his younger brother Samuel, had a building and carpentry workshop employing five men behind the cottage. The family business was in turn taken over by his son Thomas John Long, in the 1870s. Although the shoemaker George Wallace took over as postmaster in 1861, Lydia continued to run the grocery store with her daughter Maria until she died just short of her eightieth birthday in 1873. The 1881 census shows that Thomas John's sister Eliza Sophia was the sub-postmistress when the shop had also become a telegraph office, a savings bank, a government annuity and insurance office as well as a fancy stationer. By 1893 Thomas Charles Long, a great nephew of John, also a carpenter and joiner, was the sub-post-master, along with his wife Kate Annie, who was the postmistress. Née Denman, Kate was the grand-daughter of James Denman, who from 1836 was parish clerk at St Peter's and collector of the church rates for 36 years. It is likely that the building business had been taken over by George Hughes by the early 1900s. He was to be associated with many of the houses in that part of Petersham, and had probably worked as an apprentice to the Long family. Thomas Charles continued as the sub-postmaster but the 1911 census shows that he had moved to Radnor Gardens in Twickenham, where he was still listed as a carpenter, thus ending the Long family association with Ivy Cottage.

When Martha Susan Lee was sub-postmistress in 1905, a telephone service had been added to the telegraph office. Martha lived with her husband Samuel in the northern half of the building, which was known as Columbine Cottage, until 1924, after which time there was no longer a post office here. George Hughes and his family were next door at Ivy Cottage, which they occupied until 1938, with the workshops behind the house.

The small wooden single-storey shop was badly damaged by a high explosive bomb in the Second World War, making a deep cavity in the road, also causing severe damage to the house. Fortunately, Mrs Hughes, who was sheltering in an Anderson shelter in the front garden, escaped injury. Thereafter the building was known as Petersham Hollow. The cottage was bought by George's son, Roger, also a builder, in the 1949 Dysart Estate Auction. He completely rebuilt both parts of the house. The shop opened after the war as a hairdresser and then a greengrocer, eventually closing in the 1960s, when it became part of the house that we see today.

VINE COTTAGES, PETERSHAM ROAD

The first Vine Cottage was built at no. 191 Petersham Road, at a right angle to the road, in about 1820 by Sir Henry Englefield (who lived on the other side of the road at Elm Lodge) for his servant James Ferrant. Sir Henry gifted the cottage, together with 17 perches (equivalent to 85 metres of land) to Ferrant for life. Three more cottages with stabling were built on the land in 1861. At the time this photo was taken in 1907, the cottages and land had been purchased by the Earl of Dysart, along with Elm Lodge, Woodbine Cottage and Willow Cottage. All were subsequently listed in the Dysart Estate Auction sale of 1949; the three Vine Cottages as each having two bedrooms and two living rooms with a WC and an outside communal washing facility. Now the cottages have a painted white finish.

On the extreme right of the photo is GEM Palace, also known as the Coffee House or Mission Hall. The name comes from the initials of Gertrude Emma Master of Montrose House (further north on the Petersham Road), who help to found the hall in 1889 to promote the 'spiritual, moral, intellectual or social interests' of the poor of Petersham. Gertrude Master was a staunch teetotaller and a devotee of animal rights. She was the wife of John Henry Master who had retired early, having served as a collector and magistrate in the Madras Presidency in India. She had a very strong character and was also an ardent philanthropist. Her grandson was the (notorious) British art historian Anthony Frederick Blunt, who was exposed as a Soviet spy in the 1970s. He was the son of the Masters' youngest daughter, Hilda Violet, who had married the vicar of St Andrew's Church in Ham, the Revd. Arthur Stanley Vaughan Blunt.

In 1923 the Mission Hall was taken over by West Heath School, a private school (situated in the building now known as the Cassel Hospital on Ham Common), and as a Girl Guide centre and renamed Trefoil (clover leaf) House. It has been used since as the Women's Institute, a refuge for pupils of the bombed-out Russell School at Petersham Gate, a church hall and a youth club. After this photo was taken the hall was converted into flats.

WILLOW COTTAGE, PETERSHAM ROAD

Willow Cottage, 252 Petersham Road, between Woodbine Cottage and Whorne's Place was built in the early 1800s, possibly onto an older and much smaller dwelling. The house had a striking resemblance to Myrtle Cottage (see page 80). For fifty years, from 1867, the three-bedroomed cottage with its old pantile roof had, as well as a bake house, an attached single-storey bakery shop. It also had a separate granary at the rear of the house. The Census shows that in the mid-1800s, Peter Wallace lived and ran the bakery here with his son, also Peter. Peter senior died in 1869 and is buried at St Peter's. Shortly after this photo was taken in 1905, the bakery closed and the cottage became the home of the Arnold family, who lived here for almost fifty years.

In December 1988, the house was illegally demolished by the owner of Whorne's Place, (once known as the 'Old House') next door who had recently bought the cottage to extend his property. Not only did the cottage have a Grade II listing, it was also in the Conservation area and the demolition caused local outcry and some coverage in the local paper. The owner was taken to court by the Richmond Borough Council for unlawfully demolishing the house and agreed to rebuild the house, which he did the following year in the style of Whorne's, a re-creation by the American architect Blunden Shadbolt of a house by the same name which was built in about 1487 at Cuxton, near Rochester, for Sir William Whorne, then Lord Mayor of London.

209 – 233 PETERSHAM ROAD

This view of the west side of the Petersham Road, opposite Whorne's Place, with the two ladies in Victorian dress walking along the pavement, was taken at the end of the 19th century and is remarkably unchanged today, apart from the busyness of the road.

In the 1750s there were just four cottages here. By 1819 there were seven, and now there are thirteen. The single-storey pitched roof building with the odd-shaped chimney on the right is now a double-storey unit, no. 209. Nos. 211 and 213 date from c.1850. Nos. 215 and 217 (with the boarded wooden façade and slate roof) are the oldest houses in this group and date back to the first half of the 18th century. In 1746 a licence was granted for a public house here, which was known as the Horse and Groom. There are apparently still old brick inglenook fireplaces in both houses, which were common for taverns of the day.

The next unit of four houses, originally called 'Park Place', nos. 219-225, is more recent, having been built in the early 19th century. No. 1 Park Place was a lodging house from about 1870 run by the Aldrich family. The Kelly's Directory shows that Mrs Julia Aldrich and then her daughter were also laundresses here from about 1909 until about the start of the Second World War.

In the distance on the left are the four taller cottages, nos. 227-233, known as Michael's Place; these were built in 1850. This date is engraved on the side of the front wall of no. 233 together with the name 'Christmas Long', who was most probably the builder. I have not been able to find any relation to the Long family of builders (see page 85).

All the houses have allotment gardens to the rear, to which they have access over a public footpath, which follows the line of the ancient field path. Note the iron railings along the front of the cottages, which were removed for the war effort in the 1940s.

INDEX

PICTURE CREDITS

Maps by Jason Clark at Yellowfields pages 4, 52; Sir David Williams collection pages 10, 11, 13, 18, 24, 25, 30, 32, 47, 48, 60, 81, 90; London Borough of Richmond upon Thames Local Studies Library and Archive front cover, pages 13, 14, 17, 22, 28, 35, 39, 40, 49, 50, 51, 56, 59, 62, 63, 64, 67, 72, 73, 76, 79, 83, 84, 87, 89; National Portrait Gallery page 8; The Hearsum Collection page 9; John Clifford page 21; The Government Art collection page 27; London Metropolitan Archives page 68; Victoria and Albert Museum, Recording Britain Collection, John Sanderson-Wells pages 34, 36, 42, 43 and Edward Walker page 71; *Rural Nooks round London* page 75; Private Collections pages 41, 44, 55, 80; Watercolour by Thomas Rowlands on page 7; Lithograph by Edward Collier, page 31.

SOURCES AND NOTES

Richmond and its inhabitants from the olden time, Richard Crisp, 1866. Richmond At War 1939-1945, Simon Fowler, Richmond Local History Society. Ham and Petersham Reminiscences, Marjorie Lansdale. Ham and Petersham, As it Was, James Green and Silvia Greenwood. Ham Common and the Dysarts, A Brief and an Indictment, William H Harland, 1894. New Light on old Petersham Houses 1 and 2, John Cloake, Richmond Local History Society Journal, 1997 no. 18 and 1998 no. 19. A History of Petersham Common, F Nigel Hepper, Richmond Local History Society Journal, 2007 no. 28. History of St. Peter's Church, Petersham, Charles D. Warren. Pubs Inns and Taverns of Richmond, with Ham, Petersham and Kew, Richard F Holmes, the Echo Library. A History of Taxation and Taxes in England, Stephen Dowell, 1888, Google Books. Evelyn Pritchard papers at Local Studies Library, London Borough of Richmond. Research on the Working Men's Institute, New Road, Ham, Dr Claire Martin. Charity Commissioner's Report of Endowed Charities in the parish of Petersham, 1894.
Local Studies Library, London Borough of Richmond.
Surrey History Centre, Surrey County Council, Woking. Pigot & Co's Commercial Directories, Kelly's Directories and the United Kingdom Census Records.

I am grateful to Dick Hughes who shared his family's association with Ivy Cottage.

First Published in 2017 by Vanessa Fison, 38 Ham Common, Richmond, Surrey TW10 7JG

©Vanessa Fison, 2017

ISBN 978-1-5272-0980-0

British Library Cataloging in Publication Data A catalogue record for this book is available from the British Library

Design by Nick Avery
Printed in Turkey by Imago